CURRY FLAVOUR

ACKNOWLEDGEMENTS:

I would like to thank my husband, Hammond Rahming, for his encouragement and support while I was making this book a reality. Thanks to Lorna Goodison for her literary critique of my manuscript, for being my poetry mentor and for believing in me. Special thanks to Dr. Sandra Pouchet-Paquet and the Caribbean Writers Summer Institute, University of Miami, as well Angie Cruz and Marta Lucia, founders of Women in Literature and Letters (WILL), New York, for making it possible for me to be in workshops with Lorna Goodison. I would like to thank Dr. Erika Waters and *The Caribbean Writer* for being the first international publication to publish my poetry. I would also like to thank members of the WomanSpeak Journal Collective (Nassau, Bahamas) for creating a literary space for my Woman Words. Thanks to the members of the former Bahamas Writers Association (BWA) for their encouragement even while I was a very green writer putting words on paper.

Thanks to the following journals where some of the poems in this collection were first published: 'Footsteps in this Land', 'Zaboca Child' and 'Slavery Legacy' were first published in *From The Shallow Seas* (Havana, Cuba); 'Earth Goddess', 'Trini Tabanca', 'Love Up De Culture', 'Incarnation on the Caroni', 'Leaf-of-life Hands', 'Dreaming of Places I Have Seen' were all first published in *The Caribbean Writer* (St. Croix, Virgin Islands); 'Eve Of Creation', 'Wild Woman', 'Full Moon Healing' and 'Earth Mama's Necklace' were all published in *WomanSpeak* (Nassau); 'Woman Truths' was first published in *Sisters of Caliban* (Virginia, USA); 'Pink Sin and Yucca Blossom', 'Do Trees Ever Dream?', 'Summer Dingolay' and 'Passing Places' were first published in *Mango Season* (London); 'The Maharaajin That Was' was first published in *SAMAR* (New York); 'Steelpan in Miami', 'Carifesta Five – Rebirth', 'Curry Flavour' and 'I Am With You' were first published in *Thamyris* (Amsterdam); 'Waterfalls and Winter Streams' was first published in *Voice, Memory Ashes: Lest We Forget,* Mango Publishing, (London).

CURRY FLAVOUR

LELAWATTEE MANOO-RAHMING

PEEPAL TREE

First published in Great Britain in 2000
Peepal Tree Press Ltd
17 King's Avenue
Leeds LS6 1QS

ISBN 9781900715355

 Peepal Tree gratefully acknowledges Arts Council support

CONTENTS

DEDICATION

for Mama, Kenny, Premattee, Sally, Kamla and Karan

in memory of Ricky and Daddy

Om siddhi buddhi prade devi,
Bhukti mukti pradaa-yinee,
Mantra moorte sadaa devi,
Mahaa Lakshmee namo-astu-te.

Glory to you Mother of all,
destroyer of the darkness of
ignorance, giver of the light
of knowledge. Salutations to
you, Mother Divine, bestower
of Health, Wealth and Bliss!

– Hindu Prayer to Lakshmee Maataa

INCARNATION ON THE CARONI

1

My eyes have never crossed the black water;
kala pani of fear and change forever.
My mouth has never tasted the barracks of Calcutta,
my nose has never devoured rotting bodies around Cape Town
thrown overboard without Krishna's blessings,
without cremation on the Ganga or even
on the banks of the Caroni River.

But I have seen the ritual at Cedros Bay
on Indian Arrival Day. And for you, *Nani*
I have tasted blood as *Rawan* sliced your body
like sugarcane stalks on the fields of Usine.
I smelled your freedom swim through alligator waters
and I echoed your emancipation cries
as you gave birth to your daughters
on the banks of the Caroni River.

2

Grandmothers become granddaughters
and after three incarnations
your soul is freed once more as *ghee*
and camphor burn in the *thareeyaa* of your mouth
and the *deyas* of your ears.
I take *aarthi* from the flames of your body
wrapped in the aroma of a pitch-pine pyre
on the banks of the Caroni River.

Your soul still hovers ten and three days later
with the rhythm of *Bandaara poojaa*

when the pundit guides
your eldest son in ritual ceremony.
But your soul is not charioted away
by the Great Vishnu,
it stays with me here
on the banks of the Caroni River.
Your lifeforce curls upward, like wood-smoke;
then, like a rainy drizzle, falls upon me
caressing my full breasts, my round belly
and enters my womb
implanting new life
in the ripe richness of placenta
for your fourth incarnation
on the banks of the Caroni River.

ODE TO MY UNKNOWN GREAT-GREAT GRANDMOTHER

I heard you were the first
to belong nowhere.
Born on the wide Kala Pani
between Calcutta and Port-of-Spain
on a ship unknown.

Your parents, indentured labourers,
coolies from India,
lost their dreams of returning home
in the canefields of Caroni.

But you grew and you spoke
not Sanskrit or Urdu pure,
but broken Bhojpuri Hindi.
You prayed to Shiva
dancing on Gangetic Plains
you never saw.

Your eyes were the first to embrace
El Toucuche and Ciero Del Aripo.
You were the first to season
your curry mango with bandhania,
wild coriander, shadon beni
instead of true dhania
coriander from India.
Your bare feet were the first to claim
dirt paths from Cedros to Las Cuevas.

I have tried to reincarnate
you in my womb,
but I have failed.
My eyes are the last to gaze
upon the Scarlet Ibis
roosting in the Caroni Swamp.

My feet are the last to walk
the forests of Mathura.
My blood the last to make
red tikkaa on the forehead
of La Trinity.
My ashes are the last to belong somewhere.

THE MAHARAAJIN THAT WAS

"While Miss Rossignol, in the cathedral loft,
Sang to her one dead child, a tattered saint
Whose pride had paupered beauty to this witch
Who was so fine, whose hands were so soft."
- Derek Walcott, "Tales of the Islands, Chapter 111/La belle qui fut..."

Parosin use to live in the concrete house
Green across the road; she skin like mud colour,
And pushing it out, round, old-Indian bones;
She use to hide like a owl from daytime bright,
The breathing *soucouyant* of Malick/Morvant;
And noisy as a *lugarhoo* when she shuffle
On arthritic legs to make she messages,
In a white cotton sari stain with mildew.
Mama tell we how long time she use to see
That woman in a purple and gold sari.
Now Parosin alone in she temple house,
Humming bhajans to she dead husband and child;
And sometimes, by moonlight, a glimpse go show you,
A goddess glowing with a serene softness.

SITA AND THE FIRE DRAGON: A RE-TELLING

After Rama save Sita
from Rawan's seven heads
He ask she to walk
in the pit burning with flames

But Sita did not fraid this fire
She did know
what the fire dragon know
when it fly in the night

Is nothing like good and bad
is only life, death and life again
in the wind that carry
the dragon golden breath

To Mount Soufriere
is only life in that fire mud
borning from the vagina
of the volcano

When the dragon sneeze
like a slap of thunder
is only the dead
that does burn

On the forest floor
from the lightning torch
that fly out
the dragon nose

As the dragon laugh
flame does just rise up
from the dragon belly
so hot that it cause

The sequoia pinecone to burst open
scattering seeds that done wait
so long for this heat to come
and make them grow

Sita did know all of this
when she start walking through the fire
and when she walk out
the next side of the pit

Rama was glad
He think it mean she pure
that Rawan never spoil she
but the fire don't know

Good and bad
it only know that Sita was still alive
She wasn't dead yet
so it wasn't time for she to burn

THE OCEAN WITHOUT SWELLS

Ricky, what were you seeking
in Blanchisseuse
that sunny day?
Was it Nirguna Brahman
the ocean without a ripple
to take you to Nirvana
deep in the belly
of Maha Lakshmi
before she was born
from the poison
in the Ocean of Milk?

Did you beg Lakshmi Mata
to siphon the gramoxone
from your acid-eaten stomach
patch the holes with *penoos*
sweet first-calf-food
full of goodness to protect
the vulnerable baby cow,
and refill it with milk?

Brother, did Maha Lakshmi
cradle you in her arms
while she played the vina
and sing to you bhajans
from the Bhagavad Gita
before she left you
to rise up in Saguna Brahman
the Ocean alive with swells and waves
churned by the demons and demigods
fighting for the sacred nectar?

Ricky, did Lakshmi Mata offer you that sacred nectar?
Did you sip amrita, the nectar of immortality

after drinking the poison
in the sea at Blanchisseuse
that day you sought
Nirguna Brahman?
Did the serum give you strength
for your flight to the Alone?
Because all there is now at Blanchisseuse
is Saguna Brahman
and night-time dreams
of you seeking milk
in an ocean of poison.

SHIVA-KALI

I meditated the creation
with all the world in Brahma
my destiny in that cosmic egg
freedom in the lotus flower
knowledge bounded by the oceans
and the thousand rivers
love strong and nurturing
like mountains of placenta

And dreamt of the destruction
of a red putrid world
the death of trees that remember
a watery beginning
pulverized rocks that fed
an embryonic Kali
merciful Shiva awakening
in a cycle he must complete

And relived the rhythm
of an ancient melody soothing sitar
a baby girl looking up
at Chaan Mama full and bright
lighting a dark river valley
assured of tomorrow's sun
her future written in star paths
cycles of destruction and creation

JESUS AND BRAHMA
(The God in Me Hungry for the God in You)

There is a dream that never ends: a wheel
that bends and spins and curves: a movie reel.
The God in you, you call the Devil Child
Lucifer/Baby Jesus weak and mild
suckling at Brahma's breasts. Milk overflows
from the swollen teats, still your hunger grows.
All you can see is Lucifer's red face,
me hiding the nipples in Sanscrit verse.

Peel away the red mask, horns
See a new vision without storms:
Govind as gentle as Jesus the man,
Lakshmi as loving as Virgin Mary,
Kali as kind as the Samaritan,
Sita as sensual as Magdalene,
Hanuman as Holy as Gabriel,
Saraswati as shrewd as Queen Esther.

See the Godhead Brahma making
love to the Almighty King;
the cosmic birth in the lotus flower;
you and I as no less sacred lovers.

Jaya bhag-watee devi namo varade,
Jaya paapa vinaa-shinee bahu phala de,
Jaya shum-bha ni-shimbha kapaal dhare,
Prana-maamee to devi narar-tih hare.

O Mother Bhagawatee Devi, granter of boons,
Glory be to you;
You are the Supreme Benefactress.
Glory be to you.
I prostrate myself repeatedly before you,
O Divine Mother, for only you can remove
the pains of existence.
O Mother Bhagawatee,
please guide me to an awareness of the
power, wisdom and abilities that are innate
in me and show me how to use them.

– Hindu Prayer to Mother Bhagawatee

EARTH MAMA'S NECKLACE

"God's joy moves from unmarked box
to unmarked box, from cell to cell."
Rumi, 13th century Sufi poet from Afghanistan.

In unmarked boxes
from cell to cell
Earth Mama threads
our spirits
like jumbie beads
in her red necklace

And when I lose
my unborn babies
She puts their stillborn selves
in little unmarked boxes
and into your cells
for rebirth

While I suckle puppies
nurse kittens
to end this ache
in my swollen breasts

In unmarked boxes
from cell to cell
Earth Mama spreads
her life force through our souls
weaved like gainda flowers
in her yellow mala

FOOTSTEPS IN THIS LAND

I search for an echo
of a voice
of a footstep
of a cry
in this land
where my mothers
my fathers
have not lived

I long for a whisper
on the breeze
in the silence
of the sea
caresses
through the centuries
of ancestral fingers
from this land

But I am alone
without a story
in this land
where my children
refuse to be born
in this land
where I have
no umbilical cord

Oh Atabeyra
Great Mother of the Caribbean Sea
Goddess of childbirth
hear my prayer
hold my hand
build with me
the tunnel
for my children to cross

So they can
bring to me
a cry
a footstep
a voice
from my ancestral spirits
in that faraway land
in the east

Mother Atabeyra
help me hear your cries
help me hear the voices
of my mothers
my fathers
so I can leave my footsteps here
in this place
in this sea
in this land

ZABOCA CHILD

De midwife bring meh screaming out,
Mama crying turd gyul, fort chile
Papa weeping, bury meh navel
string under de zaboca tree
so ah could bear fruits like
big, plump, purple pears

De pundit call meh Lelawattee
loyal, faithful, shining like de moon
hope fuh ah lorse generation so
ah could make sons tuh imitate
dat fabled phoenix an rise from drunken
cursed ashes tuh perch on El Tucuche

Buh Papa should ah bury instead
meh afterbirth under de silk cotton tree
where it would ah dance with douens
in ah backward swirl ah infertility
ah ghostly realm ah screaming dreams
dat should ah be buh nevah go be

WHEN THE MOON FLOWS FULL

Blood flows
black red,
the colour of ripe cerise,
sweet pulp that I swallow
to coat this sour regret
rising in my throat.

Blood flows
crimson orange,
shades of ackee
bulbous, swelling
waiting to burst,
to spread out,
to show off
yellow flesh like fertilized yolks.

Blood flows
purple,
like zaboca skin
when the fruit full
and it taste of
butter and milk-cream,
rich and yielding.

Blood flows,
while I beg
cerise
to show me how to stop
these colours from spilling.

Blood flows,
while I plead
with ackee
to teach me how to catch
my embryos in my womb.

Blood flows,
while I cry out
to zaboca
for the secret
of how to push back this blood,
of how to ripen
pregnant and luxuriant.

But they do not answer,
not cerise, not ackee, not zaboca.
And the blood still flows
to remind me
that I cannot plant
my seeds
as strong as ackee,
to grow full like zaboca
birth red black like cerise.

SONG for Marina and Lindy

All Hallow's Eve
as witches gather
and goblins scatter
two hearts cry at Hecate's crossroads

While Sappho's tears bathe her sisters
across millennia
the mermaid and the rose
strum each other's heartstrings
their bodies like holy temple guitars
till a chorus of running chords
splits the silence
of a normal night
like a burst of fireworks
on Halloween

When bean soup and pumpkin pie
may satisfy Hecate
but cannot fill the hunger
of a fifteen year old promise
waiting to be consummated
waiting for the wall
to crack and fall

And saddened by the wedding card
that never says their names
nor their mothers' names
because they partake of Sapphism
because they fill their bellies
with flesh from other women's children

But while they wait they learn
to swim in their own tears
as goblins scatter
and witches gather
on All Hallow's Eve

THE EARRING

Yes Miranda
it was there
an earring in his ear
a gold knob in his ear

A golden thread
of betrayal
wrapped around
the drill bit spewing
forth from the hot hole
he was a lovely
child Miranda

Golden trumpets
blowing
hard proclaiming no more
innocence
shouting Miranda

   I fuck
   I screw

His hands
make threads
on the screw Miranda
screwing young girls with
firm breasts
young men with taut
butts like himself

Old men but never
old women
no Miranda
never old women

Om mano-jawammaa-ruta tulya wegam
Jiten-driyam budhi mataam warish-tham;
Waa-taat-majam waanar yooth mukh-yam,
Shree Raam dootam shir-saa na-maami.

I bow down to Shree Hanuman, possessor
of all supernatural powers, swift as
the wind, the mine of compassion,
subduer of the senses, remover of all
difficulties, who is unmatched in
strength, power and wisdom.
Lord wherever you are there is victory,
there is understanding, there is peace,
there is perfect harmony.

– Hindu Prayer to Shree Hanumanji

RACCOON ROADKILL

Raccoons looking like tabby cats
Die searching for food
Dead bodies line highways
In this roadkill season

Road litter carcasses
Do not speak of tiny paws
Cleaning fruit in rainwater pools
Wild eyes bright as marbles

Bright as the nine-year-old child's
Before she was ripped open
By her male relative
Before she became roadkill

But roadkill is only garbage
To be swept from our doorsteps
And buried in compost heaps
Like a cruise ship full of gays

Roadkill, highway slaughter?
Are you mad? It's just raccoons
And   little girls   and   gay men
And lesbians   and   me   and   you

A DREAMLESS MAN

I wanted to be an accountant
But I did not have the money
To pay for the privilege.

I became an engineer
But machines stole my dreams
And now I'm broke.

I would like to be
A marriage counsellor
But my wife just asked
For a divorce.

So, now dreamless,
I'll just sit on the beach
And snatch the fish
which swim past me.

CARIB WOMEN AT LEAPERS' POINT

It was in July you fed ripe
orange *poison wood* berries to your babies.
Then you drank *poison wood* bark tea,
strapped your babies to your backs
and walked to Leapers' Point
high above the surf crashing
against slippery rocks.
You flew
back to the Orinoco River,
the Amazon jungle
like toucans returning home to roost;

Away from the pearl fisheries of Trinidad
where your grown sons lay beneath
the mirror Gulf of Paria.
You flew away from gold mines
in El Dorado, silver pits
in Carthagena, where gold and silver bracelets
became manacles around your wrists.
Away from measles and herpes,
gifts the strangers brought to you
in exchange for your Guanahani.

Now, everyday in July,
I look down
at the *poison wood* berries
decorating lonely roadsides
then up at grey storm cloud skies.
I feed the child in me
orange berries
and send her flying to Orinoco.

LAS VEGAS – LAND OF THE ONE-ARMED BANDITS

The old Paiute shaman woman
who walks with the moon
in the valley of the meadows
hears in her visions
a strange mantra

twiing, twim, twim
ping, pong, twiing
twim, twim, bing, bong

A metallic mantra unknown
that she knows one day
when the Daytime Goddess awakes
over Sunrise Mountain
will drown her own prayer chants echoing
in this lake-bed valley
sheltering mesquite and cottonwood
and Paiute babies

The Paiute medicine woman
who walks with the moon
sees in her dreams stars twinkling,
on adobes higher
than Black Mountain she sees these
rainbow coloured stars

Chasing each other round and round
running to escape
the Sun Goddess who swallows the stars
in her flaming white yawn
but when the Goddess goes to sleep
the Paiute woman
sees them again, the rainbow stars
that never die sucking
life from dying Paiute babies

The old Paiute priestess
who walks with the moon
stumbles over tumbleweeds
her eyes damming her tears
like the dam she dreams will block
the Colorado River

She hears this river screaming
mingled with ghost cries
of dead Paiute babies
and big men wailing
in golden adobes
waiting to die after chasing
and losing the pot at the end
of the rainbow stars
to that strange mantra

twiing, twim, twim,
ping, pong, twiing
twim, twim, bing, bong

that unfamiliar song
of one-armed bandits

SLAVERY LEGACY

Granpa wanted
Slavery
But first
She made him

Lash my granma
Blows broke
Her skin
As Slavery watched

Smiled
Then she took him
For bitter
Sweet love

Granma licked the pus
From her putrid sores
To cleanse the source
Of her misery

Mama called it lore
Papa sneered at it
But gave birth to me
A twisted ugly animal

Then Granma
Told me black
Brutal story
Of a woman

Named Slavery
And called me
Her legacy

Om
bhoor bhuwah swah
Tat savitur varenyam
Bhargo devasya dheemahee
dhiyo yo nah prachodayat

Om, Supreme Divine, you are the Creator and Sustainer
Of all, of earth, space and heaven. We adore your pure
Radiant form – the source of all existence. We meditate
Upon your divine radiance. Inspire all our thoughts,
Guide our soul, open our inner eye – the eye of wisdom.

– Hindu Prayer – The Gayatri Mantra

REAL LIFE

Cat broke down
Car wouldn't start
Is Christmas Day
Vet cyar come
No family
On de island
No money
In meh pocket
No food on meh table
No present under no tree

Is big recession
In ninety-one
Cyar fine no work
An ah begin tuh tink
Dis is real life
De love, de smiles
De happy times
Was only fantasy
Now gone like de red
Sweet roses you used

Tuh bring meh
Den de cat come
Wobblin beggin
Fuh meh love
Ah bury meh face
In she soft, white fur
An feel ah strong
Real emotion
Ah smell de happy times
Like rosy smiles

Ah feel de love
Like arms aroung meh
An ah remember
If work, food
An money come
Or doh come
Ah go forget
Dis pain today
Buh ah go nevah forget
De only real life
De emotional fantasy

34 YEARS LATER (CUBA 1993)

Darkness descends.
Christmas-tree-lights city,
Cuidad de Habana ascends.
No lines of moving lights,
no cars of racing rats.

While in the *solar*,
luxuries are bicycles
and precocious progeny
solicit chiclets.

Hidden from *turista* eyes,
hidden behind contemptuous mosaic walls
and classical Corinthian columns
supporting half-breed poodles
on baroque balconies,
soft moonlight bathes
baby hips – bone and skin
gyrating to the music
of Ogun's anvil,
the songs of Yemaya's
sea people
and the rhythm of
Oshun's dulces aguas
with the strength
of Chango's machete
fired by Ron Varadero
and Habana Cigar.

Rivers of revolution
snake through
viridian valleys
and granma's eyes grow old
while she waits for Ellegua

to open the closed roads
blocked by Torricelli's Bill.

In the banana groves,
on the roadside,
she waits for the tourists,
the dollars,
oil for her lamp,
light to banish
the darkness
of deprivation,
of isolation,
for the chiclet
children
to rise and glow
like La Habana de Vieja.

BATTLEFIELD FOR FREEDOM

This pen

my sword flashes
slays jumbies
night/daytime ghouls
on this sheet
pristine clear
battlefield for freedom
bloodied with black
words

poems

slither around
the undersea world
of my mind
submarines jettison
torpedoes through my eyes
shatter cataract stillness
and newborn vision screams
in that first breath

short short stories

blast forth at Mach speed
Harrier jets swoop in
for the kill swift and sure
corbeaus, death's companions,
rip worldly trappings
of useless flesh exposing
bleached hollow bones
conduits of truth

my words

on this battlefield
I write
with this gun
I fight
for my freedom
with this pen

DADDY

I wish I didn't disappear
in this land where you
have never known me
as your daughter.

Daddy, can your spirit smell
this grouper-scented water?
Hear it lapping at this limestone-coral rock
brown with algae
fringing this low tide
sea mirror of a silver sky
like a barracuda flash?
Can your soul, Daddy,
see the horizon fade
into this sky like how sometimes
I vanish into cracks
in this rocky earth?

Cracks, Daddy,
like on a salt pond
when the air is so dry it thief
the water from my nose
the moisture from my lips
leaving them grey and cracked.
Sometimes, Daddy,
I disintegrate in this land
where redheaded woodpeckers wake
me in the morning
where in February the leafless
woman-tongue tree shimmers
with golden pods
like a Christmas tree trimmed
with gold coins.

And Daddy, I wish I had
a real gold coin
for every woman-tongue pod
hanging on that tree
so you didn't have to die alone,
in the old people home.
But it was you, Daddy,
who proved
you could get stupid drunk
hovering over life's gutter
like a blue-fly drinking
from a rotting hairy-mango.

It was you, Daddy,
who showed me how a man
with a half-burn firewood
can crack
his wife's head open,
their children watching;
and how a family
can dissipate, splattering reality
like how the blood from the crack
in the woman's head sprays
the walls.

Still, Daddy, I wish
you didn't have to disappear
from my life,
while I was here slipping
into cracks where you never buried
my navel string,
but where I bury my roots anyhow,
like full, red, sweet-potato slips.

LEAF-OF-LIFE HANDS

When we were babies

You fed us hot *lemon-grass* tea
To ease our colds and flu

You bathed our heads with *Limacol*
When our skins burned like desert air

With sensitive fingers you squeezed
Warm *leaf-of-life* juice into our aching ears

You satiated our hunger
with *roti* and *dhal*

Rubbed our wheezing chests
With heated *soft-candle*

You sang to us
On full-moon nights

And rocked us gently
In the *crocus-sack* hammock

But where were you, Mama?

Where were your hands
Your herbs, your songs?

When your first daughter
My big sister needed them to protect her

She was twenty years old and being kicked
By your first brother

As your mother watched
Where were you Mama?

Where was the *lemon-grass* tea?

To warm us when we lay cold
Alone on wooden floors?

Where was the *Limacol* to cool
Our burning faces damp with tears?

Your fingers squeezing *leaf-of-life* juice
On the painful abscesses growing in our hearts?

Where were the *roti* and *dhal*
We needed to plug the holes in our bellies?

Our congested chests wheezed
Longing for *soft-candle* rubs

Songs about the full-moon
And soothing hammock rocking

Because you had already left us
Nine years earlier

Where were you, Mama?
Where were your *leaf-of-life* juice hands?

Your *lemon-grass* tea breath
Your *dhal* and *roti* smell?

Your *bhajan* chanting voice
To rock me steadily to my sleep?

Jayanti manga-laa kaalee, bhadra kaalee
kapaali-nee,
Door-gaa kshamaa shiva dhaatri swaahaa
swaahaa namo astu-te.

I bow down to you, Mother, again and again,
Your name is Jayanti, giver of victories;
Your name is Kaali, the dark One;
Your name is Durga, cosmic energy;
Your name is Swaahaa, Divine Fire.
O Divine Mother Kaali,
Be gracious unto me and keep your protective
shield around me night and day.

— Hindu Prayer to Maha Kaali

MOTHER KEVA

With humble housepaint
She dabbed and blotted and washed
No one could see the pattern
The abstract painting
Mother Keva was creating
On the blank canvas of a newborn land

With hands molding clay
On a potter's wheel
Mother Keva sculpted
Young minds and glazed
Them bright with dreams
Enough to lead a nation

Her tender voice commanded
Rebellious teenage hormones
And guided lithe bodies to hilltops
Where soprano voices rang clear
Joyful like a Christmas carol

They came from the Abacos to the Exumas
Long Island to Cat Island
Inagua to Eleuthera
And Mother Keva's fingers knitted
Their unruly fibres
Into blankets of excellence

Now, twenty-three years later
The artist has covered her canvas
The potter has stopped the wheel
The teacher has erased the board
The knitter has laid down her needles
She will dance in her garden on Johnson Road

But in the Big yard
She has left behind potters spinning their own poems
Teachers crafting their own history
Knitters weaving their own patterns
Artists painting their own stories
All vibrating with rake n'scrape rhythm from Mother Keva

WOMAN LOVE

I love you
one man, two man,
three man and more
in my temple's altar
so they jook me up with silver spears
a jamette a La Diablesse

I love you
with your breasts
satisfying as a calabash mango
your round belly
comforting as a feather pillow
so they pelt me with river rock
for repeating Sappho's words

I love you
reaching deep into my womb
I snatch you from your placenta
to spare you
becoming me
and they burn me
a baby killer in the chulha

I love you   I love you   I love you
but all I get is
death   death   death

Yet the spears
the river rock
and the chulha will never kill
this woman love

EARTH GODDESS

Chinnee bite yuh
Jack Spaniar sting yuh
Gobar smell in yuh armhole
In yuh hair
An make yuh shame

Chile rotten in yuh belly
Yuh big, corrup belly
Yuh lie
Yuh tief
An yuh kill.

Rain fall las nite
River flood
Dis mornin before sunrise
She ooze out
De slitherin, slimy silt
of Nariva.

She skin sorf
Like ah baby
She colour yellow-ochre
Like de silt dat born she
She hair black
Wavy like de sea
She eyes brite
Twinklin like de sun
On de mornin water.

She look at
She reflection
On de shimmerin
Mayaro Bay
Full ah promise an life

She laff.

Jack Spaniar eh bite she
Chinnee eh sting she
Yet...

WOMAN TRUTHS

Woman things
Of womanhood
In woman heart

I hide these truths
Under the bed
Among cobwebs
Encased in dust
Like panties soiled
With dry blood
Of first period

Flimsy nothingness
Stiff with dirty
Brown fear
Hidden for years
Forgotten in
Dark musty corners

Spider-like hands
That grabbed my
Groin my breasts
Tongues like leeches
Which clung to my
Lips in lecherous
Love-clothed lust

But the bruised
Lips breasts groin
Could never mirror
The slashes
On my soul
The silenced anger
Of shattered trust

Until one day
I become brave
Daring pulling
The bed I
Expose the dust
Cobwebs and soiled
Panties of truths

The woman things
Which burst out
Of my woman heart
Shrieking shuddering
Wild like demons
In the sunlight
Of my womanhood

SURVIVAL FIRE

Fire burn in de lan
jus like de one
burnin in meh soul
how it start
why it start
nobody care

But it here
in de pine barren
scorchin, cracklin
ritual dancin
wile abandon
destroyin weh it gone

Slitherin fowl snakes
jus like slipp'ry men's tongues
promisin de bottoms
ah dey bottomless hearts
roast in dey skins
meh fire too fas fuh dey speed

Centipedes scamper
jus like vile scyamp-men
who tief in broad daylite
wit piety in dey face
den run from yuh
wen yuh fine dem out

Giant rats right weh
dey sit tun intuh charcoal
too fat from feeding
orn de weak tuh run
jus like lickerish sweet-men
who prey orn feeble women

De fire ragin orn
clearin de slime ah de undergrowt
an jus like de pine cone
need fire fuh new life
dis fire in meh soul
is meh promise fuh survival

WOMANISH TONGUE

Soucouyant
is a woman who live
by words she suck
by night from the ones
who suck her blood
by day

Womanish words
from we who drink words
like blood we drink
and we grow trees
and children with our blood

Our words
that come spilling
from mouths red with blood
mouths that want to shout
like a banshee
in the night wailing
at the full moon
so orange-eclipsed

Like her voice
that slithers
like a zandolie burrowing
into darkness
but emerging next day in light
mouthing/tongueing words hot
like tropical sunshine

WILD WOMAN – for Lynn

She dances
twisting steps of music
as she searches for a space
and she tries to create
a flower bed existence
with neat rows of zinnias and dahlias
round patches of pansies and shasta daisies
in a soft brown comfort earth

But the Earth Mother pours pain
from her belly in jagged streaks
of summer lightning
and cries raindrop tears
that seep into invisible cracks
in the brownness of her life
the unseen scars on the veins of her wrist
and the depthless fissures in her sanity

Raindrop tears that copulate
with blind earthworms
and send forth
battalions of shepherd needles
to stitch away the brownness
armies of prickly poppy
to carpet away the neatness
and troops of wild spinach
to reclaim the wilderness
that can never be destroyed
by rows of zinnias and dahlias
and patches of pansies and daisies

The wilderness that proclaims her freedom
to be wild to spread her wings
in a love vine embrace

of a space that is air
that we breathe for the life
that is free
and she teaches me
the ritual dance the twisting steps
of an unborn music
in the belly of the Goddess

FULL MOON HEALING

Chaan Mama, Mother Moon
sits in the sky
veiled in her *sari*,
pale yellow, delicate,
like *sari* on fresh milk.
Veiled like a virgin
she sits and smiles.
She has never been touched
as I was touched by the one
who writes his name in stone
with my blood,
the one who smiles
when my nine-year-old pain
pours forth.

Chaan Mama, Mother Moon
sits in the sky;
pale yellow, delicate, she flirts
with silhouettes of coconut trees;
caressing shoulders of mountains,
she plays her girlish games.
She has never been touched
as I was touched by the one
who laughs in my hair as I cup
my nine-year-old virginity blood
in hands
that would not close,
in hands like baskets,
open-weave, useless.
Hands stained with blood,
shameful blood, a forbidden blood,
an incestuous blood.

I promise
to keep the secret.
The secret I tie with rope;
with thick rope I bound up
this secret in my belly.
I scrub my hands
with lye but the blood
still flows and stains
blood-red my hands.
I scrub with lye
but the blood still stains
my hands.

Chaan Mama, Mother Moon
sits in the sky,
pale yellow, delicate veil,
tonight blushed with rose,
tinted with blood
I know she knows the secret
in my belly: I have been touched.
Touched by the one who writes
his name in stone
with my blood.
The one who laughs
in my hair as I cup
my blood in hands
that would not close.

Chaan Mama, Mother Moon
sits in the sky.
Chaan Mama knows the secret.
She has seen this forbidden thing,
this incestuous love,
every full moon night.
She has wept in darkness
for stains that would not wash,

for hands that would not stop
bleeding.

But *Chaan Mama*, Mother Moon
returns every full moon night
and veils me and my sisters,
her daughters,
with love, pale yellow, delicate:
a healing veil
she spreads on the hurt
every full moon night.

Om shan-no devi rabhis-taya aapo bhawan-tu
Peeta-ye shan-yo rabhi sra-wantu nah.

May the all-pervading Sweet Mother be pleased
to bless the craving of my soul, and be helpful
in the attainment of all happiness.

– Hindu Prayer for happiness.

PASSING PLACES

But we
who live in that soil
still have our invisible
passing places
like these pages of words
where we retreat
to let those we would love
slip away

You first brought me
to this country
your Highlands of Scotland
five years ago
I felt I'd returned home
at last after millennia of watching
mountains grow old and die

And in the blair
where I had hidden
in my primordial existence
I wanted you
to stop the car
to hold you
in the darkness
of the Black Isle
But my arms stayed
wrapped around my breasts
and for five years
I have wondered
if you ever knew

Now we are here again
in the Highlands of Scotland
driving from Dingwall

to Shieldaig
You tell me about
these passing places
on this one car road
from East to West

I think about all the times
we were on collision courses
like these cars
rushing in opposite directions
and how we always found
a passing place
where one of us
would step into this bulge
to let the other slip away
without touching
with no joining

Here in this land
of brown heather-covered beinns
and stark snow-capped
peaks of monroes
I weep

I see an old woman
bent huddled
from the bitter wind
scouring this Hebridean coast
dispossessed of her croft
that will now shelter sheep

She is me
standing in this passing place
in the dark northern days
never crossed by a winter sun
I stand aside

and watch you   cold
but we never hug each other
never let the fires in our souls
mingle and explode

Now I drink tea from cupped hands
eat Marks and Spencer cherry pie
on the marsh at Shieldaig
and watch you feed pastry crumbs
to hens prancing around you
like puppies on two legs

The rooster crows
and takes me back to a native land
heavy with heat
where the sun doesn't care
about us toiling bareback
on treeless roads
where there are no signs
proclaiming passing places

BLACK ORCHID for Olga Broumas and Lena

the memory haunts me
in a steamy
kitchen you show me
the star in the apple

but what i want to see
are stars,
stars born in the cosmic dust
of flesh

as tulips touch orchid
black orchid swelling
with soft rainwater
in the heat

of a tropic
rain   forest
of tangled chestnut vines
sprouting from the mound of Venus

i look at the star in the apple
and suck on the bitterness
of a star fruit
searching for my keys

i leave these scenes
in the steamy kitchen
for cool
sterile night air
scrubbed clean with antiseptic dew

haunted by the memory of you

I AM WITH YOU

"My Lord, each lover is now alone with his beloved. And I am alone with you."
—Rabi'a, eight-century Sufi woman saint.

When I caress the curly blue petals
Of the climbing bean-like plant
And I envision them
Wrapping around me
Warm and sensuous
Like a lover in the night
I am with you

When I smell the perfumed tentacles
of the passionfruit flower
And I pretend they are
Massaging my body
Feathery and light
Like the breath of my beloved
I am with you

When I see the yellow/black/purple
Bird of paradise flowers
Of the heliconia shrub
And I contemplate them
Lying against my naked form
Perfect in their asymmetry
Like the body of my lover
I am with you

When I sense the bass droning
of the Bahama hummingbird
And I fantasize
I am covered
In its rainbow-coloured gauze
Glowing as when I'm in

My beloved's presence
I am with you

When I hear the musical buzz
of the honeybee
And I dream I am sucking
A honeycomb sweet-
Textured overflowing with juices
Like French kissing
With my lover
I am with you

When I feel the monarch
And zebra butterflies
Flit past me in their rush
To drink wild lantana nectar
And I imagine they are
Your angels touching me
Like the fingers of my beloved
I am with you my goddess
Creator of my world

PINK SIN AND YUCCA BLOSSOM

June-bride-yucca-blossoms in May
when artists metamorphose us
in the spring of our lives
before summer heat drains
the colours from our eyes
and covers our sensibilities
in oceans of humidity
pressing down on our nakedness
hidden behind transparent ET masks

pink sin orange belly
brown sugar thighs
voluptuous mama
sometimes pretty sometimes ugly
bombards our emotions
till we long for a metamorphosis
pearly-oyster-white waxy petals
on a pedestal so high
above leaves so hard
with tips so sharp

thorns protecting the virgin
no human hand may touch
no devil vice can taint
alone aloft she sits
and waits for her lover
impaled on black-tipped green spears
he never comes
and she shrivels
in the yellow June heat
a dried-up-old-virgin-June-bride-yucca-blossom
never knowing pink sin orange belly
brown sugar thighs

FIRE EYES MIRRORED IN CANVAS
(For all the women who have modelled for artists)

Nude Woman your red pulses
like electricity
in my veins
you bathe me with incandescence
shimmering
from your silhouette
teasing me with shadows
in the apex
of your pyramid

I dream of you in fields
of green crab-grass yielding
to your legs' blue-tint
like washerwoman bluing
legs firm round support
like Corinthian columns
I see your mouth saucy-rude-
gal-inviting

From your eyes flames
shoot out of your canvas
past my shut eyelids
through my irises
and impinge my retina
reflecting
back to your eyes
of yellow fire
that singes my soul

EVE OF CREATION – for Antonius

The bird sings
songs of freedom
echo in the night
from the net, mesh, veil
with which we hide
the frailty of our humanness
legacy from Adam and Eve

But the Snake Goddess
slowly unveils our eyes
as the Eve of temptation
becomes the eve of creation
and shows us ourselves
as spiritual beings
Radha, Krishna
Oshun, Ogun
Psyche and Eros

African, European
East-Indian-West-Indianess
of our blue-green birth waters
under the yellow heat
from the orange belly
of our Bahamian sun erupting
in a red fiery passion
bursting the net of our inhibitions
until the cross is no longer
a burden death no longer the end
but the bridge with which we cross
the blackness
of our unfolding universe

Om namo vij-yaan roop-aaya param aananda
roopi-ne;
Krishnaaya gopinaath-aaya govind-aaya
namo namah.

I bow down to the all blissful Govind,
who is the embodiment of knowledge and truth;
whose love is limitless and who is the
form of perfection and eternal bliss.

— Hindu Prayer to Lord Krishna

COME INTO MY GARDEN

Bouquet my breasts
with bougainvillea bows

Flan my flower
with frangipani frills

Teazel my mouth with tongues
entwined like cabbage curls

Let me nibble
your scarlet plum nipples

Let me swallow your nectar thick
sugary like hairy mango syrup

Let me swirl your silky labia satiny
like coco plum flesh against my palate

Until we sprout wings like monarch butterflies
orange and black queens we drift
deep into Venus' fly trap

COME DINE WITH ME

Fire my legs in plantain flambé

Crush my fruit in pineapple bits

Sweeten my juice into switcher

Spread my buns like dough over crab

Roll my belly in guava duff

Knead my breasts into johnny cake

Season my lips with Spanish thyme

Deep fry and dip in lime

Savour my morsels of raunchy rhyme

Have an orga ni sm then drink some wine

COME DREAM WITH ME

Last night while the rain fell easy
As Lionel's love songs
I dreamt I was a honey bee
And you a rain lily
Vulva pink and velvet smooth
I brushed your stamens

And you slowly spread your petals ·
Taunting me with perfume
Offering aphrodisiac
With my long proboscis
Penetrating your nectar tube
I sucked sweet your moistness

Till you quickly furled your sepals
Stroking me with spasms
Then rain patter turned to storm claps
Of thunder that woke me
In tears I drummed/banged my headboard
As white lightning sang

You are no honey bee
Caught in that rain lily

CALLALOO WOMAN

You must have crab.
How else to tongue out the flesh
from between hardened membranes?
How else to make it crabby?

Put your pickled pig tail
to make it salt
but add a little saltfish,
the rankness does make saliva flow.

Don't forget the ochroes.
Plenty does make it slimy
so it just slide around the palate
and slip down nice in the throat.

You need a pint of coconut milk.
It must have a creaminess,
a little rich smoothness,
sweet like breast milk.

For sure you must have a bunch of bush:
silky greeness of dasheen leaves,
curly and coarse
as you run your fingers through.

Never do without a ripe goat pepper
but make sure not to burst it.
You only want the flavour,
not too much heat.

Don't burn them yet,
just make it more-ish
so they always come again
for more callaloo.

HERMAPHRODITE

Banana
Green and firm
Carailli
Round and knobby
Cucumber
Wet and smooth
These are my
Summer's bounty
The fruits in my
Foamy delta
Wetlands of
My passion
The gifts I share
With Eros
While Cupid
Is asleep
But should he wake
And shoot his arrows
I wish
That he will pierce
My squash

Banana
Carailli
My cucumber
With Aphrodite

A LITTLE LOVING

Sometimes in de middle of de day
Yuh just siddong
On a sharp limestone rock
And yuh watch love growing frilly
And regenerative
Green and fleshy
As a wonder of de world
Leaf of life

On de darkest of de dark night
Yuh lay down in yuh hammock
And yuh see love incandescing
Yellow like a candle-fly
Shooting through de blackness
Like a falling star
In a August midnight

When at de end of de day
Tiredness make yuh cock up
Yuh foot to get a lil ease
Yuh feel love
In de first-time-mama pussycat nipples
Tender and taut from suckling
Feeding just-born hungry kittens

Just when yuh think it look like
Even the sea cyar sustain life
And yuh ready to dead yuhself
Yuh could lay down on me
Hear de resonance of meh vibrating
heart pounding through yuh body
Yuh could breathe a Bahama breeze
Yuh could decide to go fishing again
After yuh take a little loving

CURRY FLAVOUR

You said it was the scent
of roasted geera in my hair

pungency of onion tearing at my eyes

bite of ginger in my ear

the crush of black mustard seeds
in my mouth

tang of turmeric on my nipples

the perfume of cardamom in my navel

bouquet of aachar masala on my fingers

taste of coriander leaves
trickling from my pores

the flavour of garlic
dripping from my lotus flower

that took you back to Fyzabad
that made you cry in your coming
for your mama's curry

Om dyowh shaantir anta-rikhsam, shaantih
prithiwee, shaantir aapah, shaantir osha-dhayah
shaantih, vanas-patayah shaantir-vish-ve dewaah
shaantir-brahma shaantih sarvam shaantih
shaantir-ewa shaantih saa maa shaantih-edhi.
Om Shaantih! Shaantih!! Shaantih!!!

O Supreme God, who is all bliss and peace,
may the waters be soothing and may the
medicinal herbs be healing. May the plants
be the source of peace to all.
May all enlightened persons bring peace to us.
May there be peace, peace, peace.

– Hindu Prayer for Peace

MAKING SOUP

Boil four cups
liquid memory
in a desert whirlwind
add a cup of crisp
autumn colour
and a tablespoon of
fresh sunset

stir steadily with
Himalayan mountain peak
season to taste
with teaspoons of teardrops
lower heat
simmer gently
for a dozen night-time dreams

until
on awakening
one morning
all rememberings
are blended and a poem
gurgles forth
from this primeval soup

DO TREES EVER DREAM?

NOTICE
DONT WALK HERE
A RASSCLOTH
COWS DONKEYS
GOATS and OTHER
ANIMALS will be SHOT
OR POUND. By order
The Prop.

From a Jamaican postcard which shows this notice painted
on a sheet of galvanize and posted on a tree trunk

Does this queen with the orange berries
ever see in she REM sleep
she chest wrap up in galvanize

rusty square concrete nails
digging into the softness
of she underbark

Does she ever dream/feel
donkeys and goats
rubbing up theyself
all over she trunk
cows grabbing up she leaves
and then sitting down
like nothing happen
ruminating all over she roots

And does she ever ketch
in she nightmares
this other animal jooking up
she belly with this notice
and pound he head and shout at him
"dont walk here a rasscloth"

84

SUMMER DINGOLAY

Poincianas are alive
saucy and flambouyant
as they dingolay
with sandflies
dancing in a fulgent
whirlwind drunk on banana
liqueur and yellow elder
wine in an early summer
morning damp with heat
when the greeness of the rain
is the green of young
full banana fingers
and the effervescent sun
rises to greet
her lover Gaia
in an embrace
showered with passionate
poinciana blossoms

DOWN HOME CHRISTMAS

When the days get shorter
The nights come quicker
We think of the Christ Child
Lying in the manger
But can you hear him
Blow that whistle
Shake dem Meggon bells

Blow dat whistle
Rush to Rawson Square
Blow dat whistle
Have a rake n'scrape
Slammin', jammin'
Down home Christmas

Fruitcake steeping
Benny cake drying
Ham still baking
Turkey stuffed and basted
And we remember the animals
Surrounding the Christ Child
Snuggled in the manger
But can you see them
Blow dem whistles
Slap dem goatskin drums

Blow dem whistles
Rush to Rawson Square
Blow dem whistles
Have a rake n'scrape
Slammin', jammin'
Down home Christmas

Stringing the lights
Across Bay Street
Buying the presents
In all of the malls
Looking for the star
Like the three wise men
But did you see them
At the side of the manger
Blow dem whistles
Dance the junkanoo

Blow dem whistles
Rush to Rawson Square
Blow dem whistles
Have a rake n'scrape
Slammin', jammin'
Down home Christmas

Poinsettia scarlet and green
Brazilian pepper berries
Red like English holly
Canada pine smelling sweet
Laden with rainbow-coloured bulbs
Spreading comfort like hay
Blanketing the manger
But can you behold the angels
Blow dem whistles
Blare dat trumpet music

Blow dem whistles
Rush to Rawson Square
Blow dem whistles
Have a rake n'scrape
Slammin', jammin'
Down home Christmas

Boxing Day morning
Fringed and pasted
Wrapped up in costumes
Warm like the Christ Child
In swaddling clothes
Cuddled in the manger
We hear Valley Boys
Blow dem whistles
Shake dem Meggon bells
We feel One Family
Blow dem whistles
Slap dem goatskin drums
We see the Saxons
Blow dem whistles
Dance the junkanoo
We behold Roots
Blow dem whistles
Blare dat trumpet music

Blow dem whistles
Rush to Rawson Square
Blow dem whistles
Have a rake n'scrape
Slammin', jammin'
Down home Christmas

MIAMI LIGHTS

The evening awakes
dressed in alizarin crimson
dioxazine purple
cadmium orange bubba lappa
she presents her night

On Miami Beach
mountains are born
in silhouettes
of daytime skyscrapers

Fluorescent diamond-studded
green-neon-necklaced
incandescent bangled peaks
littered with lights

Mercury vapour bathes
roller-coaster freeways where
cars glide and slide
like children in a waterscape park

Cruise ships flitter
eyelids
and lights like fireflies
dance in Biscayne Bay

Sodium yellow floods
this nocturnal Miami
like a spring June moontide
swelling the canals of
Coconut Grove

Drowning the harsh sterility
of this suntime city

where the eye is blinded
by Brancusi's *Bird*
in Space

When an aeroplane
sailing over Miami
catches the noonsun light

WAITING FOR YOUR EYES

One a.m.
I stare at lines
black, stark
Jumping-out-at-me lines
shape space
of this archi-crea-ture
I once thought
was beautiful

Now all I see
are forms of lines
following function
or are they function
lines following forms?
Lifeblood veins
arteries capillaries
electrification ventilation
locomotion lines

Like a graceful odalisque
whose classical beauty
escapes the physician's
probing fingers
searching for the guts
within pink slime
of engine grease
through which life flows
giving function
to lifeless form

One A M
sleep jilts my tired eyes
and slips into the bed
of a more responsive

lover
while I sit
and I wait
for my sun
to rise again

While I wait
for your eyes
tireless sleepless
to show me
beauty form
sense style
of this creation
this art
of this architecture
without lines

BETWEEN TWO WORLDS

I sit on this rock
bathed in the twilight
between two worlds

In the near distance
a sloop bobs lazily
on shimmering lazuli
Far away a powerboat
crosses the bay with smooth
graceful backstrokes

While on the horizon
suspended above Paradise
a parachute floats in Ariel's hands

Behind me a metal jungle
sprouts cars and trucks
each with its own immortal trailer
which, when the sun is low over Paradise,
pulls up an unwilling serenity
and trailers it away
in an empty powerboat
to another world of white noise
and painted concrete walls
where it is parked like a shipwreck

perched on a deserted rock
bathed in the twilight
between two worlds

Aapat-su magnah smara-nam twa-deeyam,
Karomi Durge karu-naar-na-veshi,
Nai-tach-chha-that-wam mama bhaav-ye-thaa,
Kshu-daa trishnaartaa jan-neem sma-ranti.

O Mother Durga, Ocean of Mercy, overwhelmed
on all sides with danger, I humbly call on you.
Forgive me for not remembering you before now
but it is only natural for children to think and
remember, O Mother, when afflicted with hunger
and thirst. O Divine Mother Durga of powerful
appearance and form, I beg of you to guide and
protect me throughout my life. I crave your
blessings. I bow to you again and again.

– Hindu Prayer to Goddess Durga

THE HILLS NOT DANCING NO MORE

Boom Boom Boom Boom
Bubu Bubu Boom Boom

Long before pond and land crabs
Spawned golden eggs
In Lake Killarney
The Blue Hills used to dance

Junkanoo !!

To Goombay drums

Boom Boom Boom Boom
Bubu Bubu Boom Boom

Long before the crawfish marched
Ochre orange armies
On Bahama Sound
The Blue Hills used to dance

Junkanoo !!

To Goombay drums

Boom Boom Boom Boom
Bubu Bubu Boom Boom

Long before curly tail lizard
Basked iridescent skin
On Old Fort Bay
The Blue Hills used to dance

Junkanoo !!

To Goombay drums

Boom Boom Boom Boom
Bubu Bubu Boom Boom
Long before white mangrove planted
grey legs and drank salt tears

From the grouper crêche
The Blue Hills used to dance

Junkanoo !!

To Goombay drums

Boom Boom Boom Boom
Bubu Bubu Boom Boom

Long before red rooster called
His friend the morning sun
To feast on potato bread
The Blue Hills used to dance

Junkanoo !!

To Goombay drums

Boom Boom Boom Boom
Bubu Bubu Boom Boom

Long before the seagulls screeched
Silver white arrows
Over Montague Beach
The Blue Hills used to dance

Junkanoo !!

To Goombay drums

Boom Boom Boom Boom
Bubu Bubu Boom Boom

Long before the obeahman give
Fevergrass bush tea
To brown girl jiggling
The Blue Hills used to dance

Junkanoo !!

To Goombay drums

Boom Boom Boom Boom
Bubu Bubu Boom Boom

Now the obeahman gone
Crab boil down
Crawfish stop marching
Curly-tail lizard dead

Mangrove dry up
Rooster get eat
Seagulls scavenging
Sir Milo's Highway

And the Blue Hills   the Blue Hills
Not dancing no more
                    Junkanoo !!
To Goombay drums
Boom Boom Boom   Boom
The Blue Hills not dancing no more
                    Junkanoo !!
To Goombay drums
Boom Booom   Boooom

FURRY'S SONG

Before the April showers
pink poui bloomed
fluffy and light
nearly so white
like you
that I saw in my dreams
you tittuping among blossoms
frolicking on that flower-covered
ground soft like a carpet

But where you rolled
you left behind bruised
poui blossoms
and I relived the darkness
of your scream
from another world
when marauding dogs violated
your belly
so raw

I could not save you
nor could stitches make you whole
so your soul sighed away
before almond trees cried red
when winter winds still howled
like marauding dogs
after devouring
a feline delicacy
of tender pink meat

Now April rains
bring green earth
croton-coloured foliage
railway daisies
where you danced
and purple morning glory trumpets
your song

SAPODILLA TEARS

Scent of sapodilla sweetness
weaves its way
into memories
ochre coloured
and moist
like sapodilla flesh
yielding ripe tenderness
shielding seeds silky
shiny black teardrops
more massive
more rock like
but not as bitter
as tears hidden
in sapodilla sweet
memories

ON BECOMING MERMAID/MERMAN

> This is the place.
> And I am here, the mermaid whose dark hair
> streams black, the merman in his armored body
> — Adrienne Rich, "Diving into the Wreck".

In that WATERWORLD
on your waterbed where I floated
you called me mermaid
stretched, wrapped waist-down
in a white sheet   of scales
after I'd taken
some of you after I'd
swallowed a piece of your armour
I dreamt I was a mermaid you

Not yet a merman
your oxygen bubbled upwards
each swirl we danced
each rhythm we waltzed
till the bubbles reached their zenith
bursting like us in our ecstasy
then your breath died
you were drowning
in that armour/cage your language
longing for heartstrings

Words do not oxidise
but water does
you let me give you breath
from my mouth let me keep you
in that water place let me hammer
your rusty armour and when at last
I chinked away your final chip of metal
you let us swim   mermaid/merman
streaming black into tomorrow

IN MEMORY OF JULIETTE

The amazingly operable little umbrellas
The bartender puts in your drinks
Always remind me of her.
Is it because the umbrella is of Asian descent
Made in Korea or China or Hong Kong? Like her?
She looked Japanese
Long pointed face like her father
But her sister looked Chinese
Round-faced like their mother.

Juliette had yellow skin
But one summer she played
Tennis for two months
And bragged at the end
That her skin looked like mine
The colour of brown-ochre sapodilla.
Her eyes danced her voice sang
As she relived her summer days.
And I longed to be like her.

Then the school bell ended recess.
She sat next to me in class
And leaned over.
Her breast brushed my arm.
I have never stopped longing
For that soft warmth
In my fourteenth September.

Now in my thirty-seventh September
I look at the umbrella
In my pina-colada:
Where are you Juliette –
Slant-eyed tennis player of my youth?
Where did you go when you disappeared
In my twenty-sixth year?
Was it Korea, or China or Hong Kong?

THE PHOTOGRAPH

She squints
from behind thirty-year-old creases.
Does she see her future,
me looking at her
in black and white?
From this two inch square
can she see my eyes
thirty years later
red with stale tears?

I peer at her squinting
at her future.
On the right is Pretty Child,
so loved, so full of *prem*,
who becomes keeper
of her brothers and sisters.

In the middle,
with the bad-tempered dog,
is Sugar Child,
so in need of love
and care she cannot avoid
the diabetes that will kidnap her life.

On the left is Brooding Child,
squinting, frowning
at the blinding sharpness of tomorrow.
Standing here in my kitchen I wish
Brooding Child had crawled
into the camera
and rearranged the image

So thirty years later,
I could stare at her

eyes and perceive
a baby ray of silver sunshine
reflected back to her future,
kaleidoscoping my days
in this blue kitchen.

LIFE IS A DRINK OF MAUBY

His bright child eyes simmered
His mouth curled
Against the mauby
He did not drink long enough
To get used to the bitterness
And then to taste the sweet coolness

Years later he drank gramoxone
And raged himself into the sea
Hoping she would swallow him
But the poison gave her heartburn
She retched him up onto the shore
Like a lifeless copra coconut

He died too young to have drunk
Long enough at life's mauby
Get used to bitterness
Taste the sweetness
Expect always coolness
Tiger balm on weary shoulders

Om twam ewa maa-taa cha pitaa twam-ewa
Twam ewa ban-dhush-cha sakhaa twam-ewa
Twam-ewa widyaa dra-winam twam-ewa
Twam-ewa sarwam mama dewa-dewa.

O Supreme One, personification of all Existence,
Knowledge and Bliss, you alone are my divine
mother, and you alone are my divine father.
You alone are my faithful companion and my
greatest friend. You alone are my true wealth
and my true knowledge. You are all-powerful,
All-love and God Supreme.

— Hindu Salutations to The Supreme Godhead

TRINI TABANCA – CARNIVAL '92

Home is
where heart is
in a body racked by pain
saying farewell to a
mountain range
chipping to the tassa
in the violet dawn
of a J'Ouvert morning

Wey de devil dey?
Jab-jab in black oil
brown mud and winer girl
gyrating, molesting
the Sound Tronics truck

Twelve year old
with sleepless eyes
beats out the rhythm
of a seasoned panman
on a silver oil drum
her tender baby hands
Rugged around
rubber-tipped pansticks

Dhalpurrie roti
pelau callaloo
Old Oak White Magic
Bently on a hot, breezy
Pretty-mas Tuesday
Form a line and
Wine on something
If yuh cyar get ah woman
Take ah man

Feathers, sequins
tinsel oscillate
smooth spandex sirens
rotate lasciviously
across the savannah
enticing setting sun
and mountain range
to copulate in a las lap
before Ash Wednesday
when we bathe in ashes
and pretend we sorry
we didn't let Satan
have all the fun

Now flying in de plane
above the mountain
away from this land
pain have meh crying
in meh heart
for where home is

WATERFALLS AND WINTER STREAMS

Daffodils burst forth like spawned suns
from a dying winter, heralding another spring
new life, rebirth, resurrection
and daisy-chain friendships bloom
like pale primroses on frosty ground
under a cobalt blue sky
mirror of the universe, keeper of time

But these are not mine
and what I claim are
Shepherds' needles unable to stitch
the woolen coats to warm their sheepless shepherds
allamandas with their poisoned cups of butter
untamed morning glory
snatching life from the Hibiscus hedge
and a hazy heaven of Sahara dust
in a choked tropic evening

Where the only falls are waterfalls
and summer is perpetual
where sweet spring water satisfies the thirst
and is just as cold as winter streams

DREAMING OF PLACES I HAVE SEEN

Looking out on this land
      so flat and empty
   longing for places I have seen
olive groves in the mountains of Italy
    blue lakes in the valleys of Inverness
       crystal Caura streams echoing kiskedee
         songs and red, roaring Manzanilla surf

    I cannot see the soldier crabs seeking shelter
   soft bodies scurrying for survival from shell to shell
or the fierce light of sea urchins beneath clear surfless water
        under watchful brown eyes in the swell
     of casaurina groves standing
   tall and straight like sentinels
shielding this vulnerable land

This longing for places I have seen
tugs at the invisible strings on the ventricles
  of my heart like the strings on a puppet in the play
          The old man's voice is hoarse and dull
         a puppet whose dreams became null
          who never saw the compressed cosmos
        in his backyard while longing for his chronicles
           to be relived in places he had seen
           But I shall not be like that old man

    My dreams shall be as bright as the Bahama hummingbird
     dancing, drunk on the nectar of the poor man's orchid
  till my death I shall marvel at the beauty of the symmetry
of the curly-tailed lizard and watch it close its eyelid
    as it dreams of a heaven filled with spiders
I shall frolic with the nanny goat and her kid
    in a dusty Long Island yard and spend
naked nights with balmy breezes contented
as I dream of places that I have seen

INDEPENDENCE SESTINA
– On the 25th Anniversary of Bahamian Independence

In '73 we lowered all Union Jacks
Heralding our nation's birth
With black and gold and turquoise hope
Burma Road riots crushing the years
Of the British man's flag
In July heat we spun December junkanoo dances

From the darkest caves came freedom dances
Children playing jacks
Hop-scotching in streets lined with flags
Colours showing off black birth
Turquoise seas unspoilt for immemorial years
Glorious sun showering golden rays of hope

A little black girl full of hope
For the day in her visions when she dances
After training for twenty years
Goat pepper sauce hot and not playing jacks
Even though her Mama cried at her birth
In her dreams she is wrapped in Bahamian flags

At the Olympics, Bahamian flags
Wave amid screams of satisfied hopes
And benny cake assertion of our birth
The purple seagrape girl dances
Hugging Jills and Jacks
After tumbling down hills bleeding for years

Poets write verses about the years
Red, white and blue flags
Flew high, these Union Jacks
That swatted black hopes
And bound Junkanoo dances
Before we shredded them with our birth

The day that gave us our birth
We celebrate twenty-five silver years
With Bahamian music and Vola Dances
Draping our bodies with clean flags
Washed in cerulean waters of hope
Feasting on peas n'rice and fried jacks

With brown-skinned dilly love we have given birth to this flag
Eaten corned grouper in lean years but kept always our hopes
Our dances that proclaim to the world we are no jacks

CARIFESTA FIVE – REBIRTH

I

I dream of this sea
black and brown consciousness
flowing like pitch
on Point Fortin roads
pulled by Chaan Mama
in a swollen tide
of rediscovery

but now and then
the blackness breaks
and the red belly
of the sea pushes up
through needle chooks
lifeblood of Caribs and Arawaks
Africans and Indians
buried forever in the
Caribbean Sea

out of the belly
comes pain from inhumanity
from genocide
indentureship and slavery
hidden behind carnival masks
of humming birds and hibiscus flowers
green fields and blue mountains
white sands and waterfalls
in this oildrum steelpan
reggae soca zouk
tourist paradise

II

I dream of the kala pani
and see lighted deyas floating
on this sea of darkness
dispersing poisonous snakes
spiders and tigers
unknown creatures
of the night

then like Maha Lakshmi
rising from the churning
waters in the beginning
I see bodies rising
from beneath the deyas
I see men and women
in each hand a lighted lamp
standing straight and tall
black and brown faces softened
in the flickering flame

over here I see Dessalines
over there Jose Marti
and while Garifuna and Kuna
chant life poetry
with Invader and Destroyer
Lokono and Shango
dance the monkey dance
till I dream that even
Hanuman has been reborn
in this Carifesta Five
of my Caribbean Sea

STEELPAN IN MIAMI

Last night I drove
over plain Miami
far in the Southwest
to Miami Pan Symphony
Panyard not under open skies
not bounded by mountain peaks
Cierro del Aripo and El Tucuche
but swallowed in the stomach
of a boxy warehouse

Steelpan music cornered
muffled by dense
con crete pre fab walls
not ringing out over
Queen's Park Savannah
not jingling like running water
in East Dry River

Saw the girlchild beating
six bass pans
made in one afternoon
not by Spree Simon the Hammer Man
but by Mike Kernahan
Trini in Miami

Listened to the boychild
strum the cello pan
heard the manchild
the womanchild
on the chrome tenor pans
carrying the calypso tune

Not to Maracas Bay

with coconut fronds
and six foot waves
but to Miami Beach
manmade fringed
with sea oats and coco plums

And when the music died
a farewell so warm like Miami heat
a Trini voice bidding
"Drive safe eh"
an incantation from the streets of
Port-of-Spain
a familiar song so strange
in this multilingual
Caribbean city in the frying pan
handle of North America

LOVE UP DE CULTURE

It does hit yuh
Bam! Jus so
an sometimes dis culture
does wrap arong yuh
naked body
all slinky and sexy
slow and dreamy
like it want to make
love wit yuh

at other times
it does make yuh knees
get weak
yuh trimblin all over
moanin and groanin
like yuh is a Shango Baptist
ketchin de power

an den again
sometimes it does
get yuh excited
eyes open wide
an shining like black opal
heart ponging in yuh chest
like tassa drums in a
cooking night or hoosay

but always always
at de dead ah night
in ah silver riddum
ah crooning melody
wedda Baron or Polly Sookraj
steelpan or sitar
it does climax Bam!
an jus so it does go

NEW TITLES FROM PEEPAL TREE PRESS

ELECTRICITY COMES TO COCOA BOTTOM
MARCIA DOUGLAS

Electricity Comes to Cocoa Bottom takes the reader on a journey of light, from the flicker of the firefly in rural Jamaica, through the half-moonlight of the limbo of exile in the USA to the point of arrival and reconnection imaged by the eight-pointed star.

It is also a journey of the voice, traversing back and forth across the Atlantic and across continents, pushing its way through word censors and voice mufflers and ending in tongues of fire.

In making this book a Poetry Book Society recommendation, its selector commented: 'Marcia Douglas has the kind of intent but relaxed concentration which ushers the reader into the life of a poem and makes the event – a wedding, a hot afternoon, an aeroplane journey – seem for a while like the centre of things. This is a rich and very welcome book.'

Marcia Douglas was born in England and grew up in Jamaica. Currently she teaches at North Carolina State University, Raleigh. Her first novel, *Madam Fate*, is to be published in 1999 in the USA. *Electricity Comes to Cocoa Bottom* is her first collection.

Specifications
ISBN: 1-900715-28-7
Price: STG£6.99 / US$12 / CAN$17
Pages: 66
Date of Publication: June 1999
BETWEEN THE FENCE AND THE FOREST

JENNIFER RAHIM

Comparing herself to a douen, a mythical being from the Trinidadian forests whose head and feet face in different directions, Jennifer Rahim's poems explore states of uncertainty both as sources of discomfort and of creative possibility. The poems explore a Trinidad finely balanced between the forces of rapid urbanisation and the constantly encroaching green chaos of tropical bush, whose people, as the descendants of slaves and indentured labourers, are acutely resistant to any threat to clip their wings and fence them in, whose turbulence regularly threatens a fragile social order. In her own life, Rahim explores the contrary urges to a neat security and to an unfettered sense of freedom and her attraction to the forest 'where tallness is not the neighbour's fences/ and bigness is not the swollen houses/ that swallow us all'. It is, though, a place where the bushplanter 'seeing me grow branches/ draws out his cutting steel and slashes my feet/ since girls can never become trees'.

Jennifer Rahim was born and grew up in Trinidad. Her first collection of poems, *Mothers Are Not the Only Linguists* was published in 1992. She also writes short fiction and criticism. She currently lectures in English at the University of West Indies in Jamaica.

SPECIFICATIONS
ISBN: 1-900715-27-9
Price: Stg£7.99 / US$13.60 / CAN$19.20
Pages: 88
Date of Publication: July 2000
MOTHER JACKSON MURDERS THE MOON

GLORIA ESCOFFERY

A vivid cast of characters throng these poems. There is Mother Jackson, the ole hige who lays out her thoughts like a mortician, who is both creator and destroyer. There are the players of the Rootsman Theatre of the Absurd, such as fallen politician Julian Lapith, who knows too well the power of incantation; Dub Deacon Lapith with his Sankey soul; poor Bedward Lapith with his millenarian dreams of flight; Busha Godhead self swoopsing down to intervene in human affairs and – the heroine of the cast – Aliveyah, to whom nature speaks direct by the nudge of a beak.

And there is, of course, their creator, Miss G.E., who shares with us the 'rockstone passion of a Jamaican country bumpkin born and nurtured in Arcadia'. Whether in her celebrations of domestic happiness in a house where even the chairs talk, or in her satires on Jamaican life, Gloria Escoffery writes with a visionary intensity and fantastical imagination which is all her own. And though she feels it is no joke to be three people – old woman, young girl and child – who don't quite understand one another, Miss G.E. cannot but write her love letter to the world.

Gloria Escoffery was born in 1923. She has worked as a teacher, written extensively on Jamaican art and is one of her country's finest painters.

SPECIFICATIONS
ISBN: 1-900715-24-4
Price: Stg£5.99 / US$10.50 / CAN$15
Pages: 60
Date of Publication: March 1998

Earl McKenzie
The Almond Leaf
ISBN: 9781845230128; pp. 64; 2008; £7.99

Earl McKenzie's poems are beautifully and deceptively simple, but their crystalline observations record life in all its complexity. Patricia Harkins, in *The Caribbean Writer* described his earlier *Against Linearity* as a 'book to cherish' for the particularity of its images from nature and 'his keen insight into human hearts'.

These qualities are deepened in this new collection, where the whiff of mortality demands an even stronger sense of continuance, affirmation and joy in love, family, music, art and, above all, in his beloved Jamaica. If this Eden is a fallen one, Adam has not been expelled from the garden where, with his mate, 'Together/we share the temptation of the snake/in the garden of rocks and flowers'.

In these poems of quirky, unassuming observations, McKenzie never preaches, but he does find sermons in lilies, and what he discovers for himself provides a way of wisdom for those readers inclined to look for it.